Personality

&

Blood Type

A guide to LOVE, WORK, and FRIENDSHIPS

Wendy Watson, C.Ht.

Avid Readers Publishing Group

Lakewood, California

Acknowledgements

I am deeply grateful for the support of my daughters, Serenity and Chelsea, who are constant inspirations in my life. This book was written with the assistance of countless Japanese and Korean research subjects, translators, and friends, without whom this book would not have been written. I would also like to thank my editors, Chelsea Watson and Sumaya Elahi, whose professional writing skills and heartfelt encouragement were inexpendable to me.

Forward

Americans have an insatiable appetite for understanding human behavior, as seen in the popularity of the self-help section of bookstores. The knowledge of how our blood type characteristics impact every aspect of our lives can now be used to start a new dialogue about whom we marry, befriend, and employ.

The correlation between blood type and human behavior was first studied in Japan in the mid 1920's. Today blood group information is part of the daily cultural norm in both Japan and Korea. It is pervasive throughout all mediums: websites, blogs, television, newspapers, and movies. They use blood type information in relationship building, both professionally and privately. It's embedded in the very fabric of their workforce, with blood type being included on their resumes. We have gained a lot of knowledge from Eastern philosophies in the past, and now it is the time to disseminate the information regarding blood type.

I became fascinated with blood type and its effect on human behavior in 1998 when I began to interview Japanese and Korean foreign students ranging in the ages of 18-60. It ignited a passion to research this phenomenon. Since that time I have found that Americans, as well as countless other nationalities from around the world, fit the categorizations as well as the East Asians.

People who do not know their blood type can find out by asking their physician, by donating blood, or by contacting my website.

Blissings,

Wendy Watson, C.Ht.

www.wendywatson.weebly.com

Wendy Watson, C.Ht.

Chapter One

General Attributes

O Blood Type

Ohhh, the Osssss! The O blood group is the most flexible, easy-going, open-minded, and honest of all the blood groups. They are people-people, who don't like feeling isolated, and are at their best when surrounded by friends and family. Their group bonding extends from family to friends, to the world-at-large. They possess a certain selflessness that makes them willing to sacrifice their personal needs for that of the group. The O's are bold and brave, and come to the defense of those unfairly treated. However, when treated badly themselves, they are unlikely to come to their own defense. It's the personal rights of others that trigger them into action. Although their courage of conviction prompts them to protect the downtrodden, they aren't really fighters – they're lovers. They are the romantics of the blood types, never ceasing to believe in love. With romance in their heart and adventure on their

1

minds they are always fun to be around. When it comes to success they have tenacious spirits. They venture courageously forth marching towards their goals. They are typically strong-willed, without being stubborn. The O's are competitive, but only to a point. They are as gracious when they lose, as they are when they win. They can reframe the negative and even make a defeat into something positive. They believe in the win-win philosophy and are sincerely happy for others' success. To them, life is not a zero sum game. Quick-witted and nimble-footed, they make swift choices, responding with both brain and heart. They trust both of them equally. The O's have astute people skills. They are able to easily identify other people's strengths and help them capitalize on their unique qualities, personally and professionally. The O's live life feeling free from the restraints of most of the rules; however, they do follow the ones they think are relevant, logical, and congruent with their conscience. For underlying their sense of freedom is their sensitivity to others.

A Blood Type

The calm, self-controlled A is a group with a Zen-like personality. "You are who you are, and I am who I am," says the A. The subdued emotions of the A's can be an advantage or a disadvantage, depending on the circumstances. A's are known to be the most responsible blood type and they try to do the right thing whether in quitting a job or breaking up with a partner. All is done with integrity, logic, and reasoning. Because of such diplomacy, they are the blood group that stays in touch with ex's much longer than other blood types. A's are also very discerning. Although this trait is almost always positive, the one downside is that it can lead to indecisiveness – a common trait amongst A's. This slow pace of decision-making ranges from buying shoes to selecting a mate: all details are taken into consideration before making a decision. This deliberation can be lengthy. Because A's are extremely careful in their endeavors, they may appear to be adverse to risk-taking. However, once they make up their minds to do something, they are bold and daring. They do take enormous risks, but the risks are calculated. Persistence and tenacity is key to success in their lives. If they lose interest – in something or someone - watch out - it or you may be swiftly removed from the scene. They are also detailed planners and like the intricacies of well thought-out plans. Two of the many positive traits of the A's are that they have both high self-esteem and humility. They have no need to prove themselves - to anyone. They do not boast, and have little interest in those that do. They are attracted to people with a similar sense of humility. Although they have this inner core of confidence, they are often, at the same time, self-conscious. They do not feel comfortable with all eyes on them, and will avoid attracting attention to themselves. Although they can appear outgoing, they are usually private people. A's make gracious hosts and have an innate ability to make people feel comfortable just as they are. They are wonderful party people because they are very well liked; however, if they had to choose they would opt out for a few deep friendships rather than many superficial ones. They also take a long time deciding if a new acquaintance can be a true friend. They are team players, which makes them easy to be around, both socially and in a work environment. Cooperation is second nature to them. Another wonderful characteristic of the A's is that they don't criticize other people. This is partially due to a real sensitivity to other people in general, and to a true respect for other people's ideas. They have a special gift of seeing things from all sides and understanding the diversity of opinions. They are the diplomats of the blood types and secretly hope others share this quality. Common sense is ultimately important to them. They have subtle, delicate personalities, full of grace and presence, and should be treasured for their beautiful nature.

B Blood Type

The B's are strong-minded people with personality-plus. They are ever so charming and charismatic; they can steal your heart and even knock your socks off. No surprise – they are also known to be the players of all of the blood types. They are passionate and become very attached to the special people in their lives, especially older friends. And because the B's are lovely people, their loved ones are equally fond of them. However, no matter how strong their bond is with others, B's never cater to anyone. It's just not in their nature. They are self-assured, speak their minds, and do just as they like, regardless of other people's opinions. Even though they are a confident group, they can be easily hurt by criticism. So it is in everyone's best interest to steer clear of anything that could be construed as criticism when communicating with a B. They really thrive with people who accept and appreciate them just as they are. Also, the feeling of inferiority is really out of nature for the B's, so when faced with this feeling, B's feel very thrown off, and may react by saying or doing things that are counter-productive to their real intentions. As unconventional thinkers, the B's may be less adaptable to groups and have the need to spend time alone. They do great in one-on-one friendships, and especially need time alone with lovers. Full of emotion, some extreme B's can seem like emotional roller coasters. Life with a B can be intense - there may even be a sense of the dramatic. However, even when they get upset and tempers flair, you can trust that it will be short-lived. Ultimately, they are never controlled by their anger. What's wonderful about B's is that they have an inner core that remains calm and objective. Typical B's consider themselves to be very practical, even when others think they are being driven emotionally. They do have a unique ability to be both emotional and objective. One of the most noticeable characteristics about this group is that they have a heart for causes of people, animals, and the environment. They have a broad range of interests, which they immerse themselves into with great passion. When they get involved it's all or nothing, yet still, this doesn't limit them to just one. They have the ability to pour energy and passion into each new interest as it comes along. In fact, these multi-talented people can quite effortlessly maneuver among their varied interests. Take a look at the B's and you will see that they are a passionate bunch. They are regarded to be the fearless blood group - risk-takers at heart. Living life fully is the M.O. of the B's. Carpe diem.

AB Blood Type

The AB blood group has been given the moniker genius/ crazy. Take your freak-flag and fly it! Intellectual, analytical, creative, and compassionate, they think outside the box and are strategists by nature. But they are not just all brain; they like to be around people too. One of their unique qualities is their captivating wit, which brings them many friends. They tend to have friendships with a wide range of people, not limiting themselves to one group. Although friendly, the AB doesn't always make a good first impression. They often hide their true nature until they assess the situation at hand. It isn't until they trust someone they are able to show their true selves. AB's make loyal, lifelong friends – they believe that 'a friend in need is a friend indeed'. They are genuinely happy to be of service to others. Because a major motivation for the AB's is serving others, community work and volunteering allow them perfect outlets for their energies. It is here that their compassionate nature can be expressed. AB's are not overtly sentimental. They believe actions speak louder than words. They have a strong sense of social justice and the AB should be used by society to help solve problems. They have great negotiating skills, using reason, logic, and heart. Seeing both sides of an issue, they are able to settle problems between disparate parties. With all that said, the AB can have idiosyncrasies. Though they are the most likely candidates to help someone, they are also the most likely to maintain distance in relationships. They set clear boundaries. Their privacy means a lot to them and they will go to great lengths to protect it. The AB can be a perfectionist, which may lead to stress. However, they tend to mask their tension, and generally appear calm and relaxed. Even their closest friends usually won't see through this façade. The AB also won't show how hard they work. So while they spend a lot of time doing things the 'correct' way, they also are losing sleep and shattering their nerves. The AB prefers that people only see the results of their efforts; therefore, most people think their success comes effortlessly. The AB is the blood group that is the least satisfied with the way things are – always questioning 'why'. Their intellect is always working on ways to answer their many questions, and they continually conjure up new ways to create the most ideal. Sometimes they are like A's, sometimes like B's, and sometimes a brew all their own. With an artistic, giving nature, wrapped up in a logical, witty intellect, the AB is a blood type that gives the world both more character and more joy.

Chapter Two

How To Love Them

The O Blood Type

Take No For An Answer

The O blood type is flexible, so they often go along with what is happening. But make no mistake, they can be perfectly blunt and can make things explicitly clear to someone when necessary. When they really mean 'no' they say it very directly. If you get the idea that they really aren't interested in you, giving up may be your only option. The O's often have a gregarious nature, but if you aren't their style, an O may not even know you are there. If you are not on their radar, there is a reason for it, and after an attempt or two at gaining their attention you shouldn't persist any longer. This is the time to take 'no' for an answer. When they say 'no', they mean it. However, if you feel that the O is receptive to you, go for it!

A Good Word

Since O type people have a tendency to have a strong sense of self worth, honest flattery is the way to their heart. They will be glad that you noticed all of their positive attributes. You should ask them how they are feeling about life in general, and in the relationship specifically. They come from a place of wanting to know how you are really feeling, and O's would like to think that you care about their feelings as well. So when they ask you about your feelings, be open and honest because sincerity makes them feel intimate with you. Now you have their attention and you can be part of their inner circle.

Compatibility

Most O's are very agreeable people and like to have compatible relationships. They don't enjoy arguing with people - over the little things - or the big things. If you find that the O type starts to insist on something, regardless of its validity, it's not a bad idea to listen and avoid starting a disagreement over it. Feeling that you understand them means a lot to them. Give it your best shot, and don't be surprised when you find that they'll meet you at least halfway if you give them a chance to be heard first. After they mull things over, they might even agree with you. Another important tip with the O's is when you give them advice, make sure it doesn't sound like a lecture. O's don't like being told what to do, especially in condescending tones. That kind of approach only offends them and it might make them shut you out completely.

Commitment

They are quite single-minded when it comes to relationships. Their weakness is the person who is 100% committed to them. It's very believable for an O when you say that he/she is your true heart's desire. Some people think that this makes them naïve, but it's really that they believe in the purity of the heart. Because you've proven to them that you think find them irresistible, they might reward you with their loyalty. But we know that the game of love is a delicate dance, so by the same token, you may want to subtly let them know that other people desire you as well. If the O realizes they have some competition they will likely be more drawn to you. Just make sure that you don't trigger jealousy because it could backfire on you! You should always assure them that they are your first priority. And another tip: don't talk about the positive attributes of the people who they conceive to be competition. They don't take well to being compared to others, and especially in a fragile relationship. That could be the straw that breaks the camel's back. When you show them that you only have eyes for them, they become putty in your hands, leading you both to love and fun.

The A Blood Type

No Pressure

When you want to get close to an A, go ahead and make a move, but don't force their hand. If you pressure them into making a decision about you, you just might find they will back off. It's not a good idea to hurry the A type; they need time to get close to you. They have incredible discernment, and it's unlikely that they'll give their whole heart to you right away. You need to go through all the steps: get to know them and reveal all your sides, allowing them to see who you really are. They are very calm, cool and collected, but don't confuse this with being cold. They are warm, and ready to love the right person, even if it may take more time than some other blood type. They love integrity and maturity, and they check to see if those traits show up in you. Another attraction for the A is a person's consistency. They have great respect for consistency; if you can't give them that, they may shut you out of their lives for good.

Happiness

The A type person always tries to make other people happy – it's just in their nature. The key to their heart is being that same type of person. A's are especially appreciated for making others comfortable at social settings. Kindness, gentility, and politeness are the calling card of an A, and they expect the same behavior in return. All this enables them to reach their happiness quotient. An A is lots of fun to be with and they can be really funny, so a way to their heart is to share laughter. A daily dose of laughter could seal the deal with them. Having the same sense of humor is really relevant to the A's. They don't like mean-spirited jokes and won't tolerate it. When you are trying to win the heart of the A, or keep their love, remember that good conversation is part of being with them. They don't like it when the conversation has an awkward pause in it - they think it is impolite. Although the A is not necessarily a big talker, they are very gracious and think that it's just bad form. They truly love great conversationalists, so talk about a broad range of topics and share your ideas with intelligence and passion. It's a sure way to capture the heart of the A.

Feelings

A's feel satisfied when they are sure that their partner really cares about their feelings. The A will always appreciate when you remember the little things they say or do. It shows them that you are a sensitive person with the depth of soul that they need in a mate. It's also important for you to be considerate of their friends, family, and other important relations.

Discretion

Discretion is of the utmost importance to the A. They dislike people who lack tact, whether it is making unwarranted comments, being too direct, or ignoring others. They are very sensitive to rudeness. One thing is for sure and that is the A's are true diplomats, and will never embarrass you. On the other hand, it would be very easy to embarrass them in public. So if you want to win their respect, check your tact-ometer. They are very aware of their surroundings and are polite to the point of self-consciousness. On a date, an A is happiest somewhere private and cozy. They don't need to be seen at the hot spots; in fact, they are less comfortable when all eyes are on them, and you'll find that they generally act more reserved in public than the other blood groups. That said, don't misunderstand, the A *does* desire great gestures of love, just in a more low-key kind of way. Never give up in trying to please them in the specific ways that they need to be pleased. The A's love is worth it!

The B Blood Type

Contact

One of the strategies for catching the attention of the B is quite simple: make contact often. B's are communicators and they want to hear from people they like, so text, email, or call them. Just do it! The B feels appreciated and valued by the close contact. Don't worry about bothering them because they will just ignore you if they don't want to hear from you. They have no problem discounting people they don't like very much. They are the blood group that loves socializing with friends and family on a regular basis. However, don't be surprised if it's on their own time. Whether they are busy or resting, they have a "B-kind" of inner clock that the world just has to adjust to. But make no mistake - being a visible entity in their lives is a sure way to show them that you care for them, and that means a lot to the B who has a sentimental nature – a nature they don't show in an obvious way. Being accessible and available is key in winning their heart.

Praise

The sky is the limit when giving praise to the B's - they can handle it. Just as the A needs a daily dose of tender loving care, the B's can use a little positive reinforcement on a daily basis. This is especially true when they are feeling a little low. If you want the B's to know you care about them, give them a lift by sharing your positive thoughts about their good traits. They will remember you were there for them when they needed it and they are able to bounce back more easily with a little help from those who care for them. If they are feeling isolated and alone, your reassurance and support brings them back to their senses. Although they are normally positive people, in these times, they really need your encouragement. Here's your opportunity to make them feel confident again and remind them just what delightful people they really are. The B will reward you with gratitude, and just maybe, enduring love.

Spontaneity

The B loves to be surprised - so be ready to take a trip on the spur of the moment! Someone who can pull this off perfectly will surely capture the attention of the B. Hanging around just waiting for something to happen doesn't impress them much. Showing them how you can surprise them with an impromptu new venture wakes them right up. They live in a fast paced, yet, smoothly functioning world. Try showing them something fun and off the beaten track. This really intrigues them. And take note: most B's are epicureans at heart, which means they are thrilled if you show up with something delicious they have never tried. The B is always ready for the new. If you want to really make the B happy, give them what they want – a life full of great surprises.

The AB Blood Type

Passion

AB's see life on a large scale and love with great passion. They live life in a romantic storyline, searching for the ideal mate. Partly with their heads in the clouds, and partly with their feet on the ground, they look for passion and practicality. They have many stipulations for their passionate love, and protection and security are two of them. Take good care of them and they will take good care of you. Listen to them, love them, and protect them, and you will feel their passion in return.

Loyalty

The inner core of a person is what really counts to the AB, although they appreciate the outer beauty of a person, as well. When all is said and done, they are 'looking for a heart of gold' and they will search for a lifetime, if they have to. Never settling for someone who is less than true-blue, an AB can't stand hypocrisy. Sincerity wins them over every time. But keep in mind, if you betray them, they will never trust you again. So it's game over at that point.

Finances

Money matters are a key factor in winning the favor of the AB's. They consider economic stability paramount. They see money handling as a reflection of overall character. Their love is full of romance, but they love their partner even more when they see that they are able to manage money, rather than the money managing them. They just see money as an extension of the self.

Friendships

One way to the heart of the AB is through their friends. AB's usually have great, loyal friendships, and what these close friends say about you matters to the AB. If friends rave about you, it will likely sway the AB in your direction. The opposite is also true. If their friend's impression of you is bad, suffice it to say, it will not bode well for you. Winning over the AB's trusted friends will put you one step closer to getting the AB heart!

Partner

Be the AB's partner in play! Whether sports, games, or hobbies, your role as their equal companion will increase their feeling of closeness with you. An AB lover falls hard for the partner who is as much fun as their friends. They will find themselves feeling a connection with you like they have never felt before with a partner. Passion and play are the keys to blowing their minds and winning their hearts. As both best friend and lover, you will be impossible to resist.

O

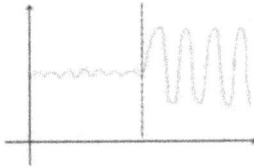

O's handle stress until the breaking
point and then they erupt.

A

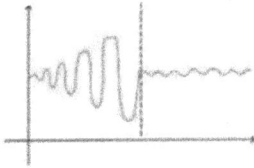

A's have a little stress all the time
and then in a crisis they are calm.

B

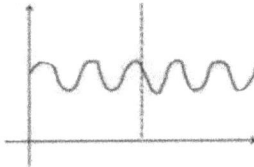

B's are up and down through the day
and don't change with externals.

AB

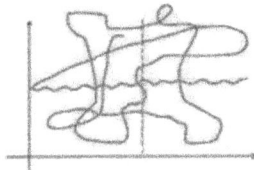

AB's are unpredictable, being calm or
stressed throughout the day.

Chapter Three

At Work

O Blood Type

Leaders

The O's have many talents, and use them to their fullest extent. They are hard working, tenacious, and are not afraid of trying new things. As a leader they are individualists, remaining true to themselves, and yet at the same time keeping in mind other people's needs. You will find that most O's are confident and decisive, trusting their minds, as well as their hearts. They will make personal sacrifices for the group, and believe that the only true success is when everybody benefits. They value the win-win business model. Power and prosperity can often be focuses of O's; however, honor and justice are just as important to them. One of the most obvious qualities of an O is their optimism and cheerfulness. As a leader they have a natural inclination to make friends easily and often view their company as a family.

Workers

The O is a great colleague to have at work, as they are usually in good spirits. They like to be liked, and have a broad range of friends. The O's ability to get along with others is often the glue that keeps people together in a work environment. They genuinely care for others, and make social connections through sincerity and honesty. The downside of their honesty is that it can unintentionally hurt someone's feelings. As much as they are great at connecting to those around them, there will always be someone who feels slighted, and this could become a problem for them. If it does manifest to an uncomfortable situation, the O rarely holds a grudge so the working relationship can be maintained. Their optimistic outlook allows them to try many new things, and even if it doesn't work out, the O is not disheartened. They can move on to the next project with ease. They are able to multi-task and take action with lightening speed. But just like with their honesty, their speed can be a double-edged sword. The work gets done quickly, but some co-workers can find them abrupt. Regardless of these potential negatives, the O's supportive nature makes them well- liked. Service to others is a motivating force for an O, and when in this service mode, the O is perseverant in getting the job done. They are motivated by purpose, but if their purpose becomes blurred they lose their will to work completely. The O is energized when surrounded with other people's energy. They can work alone, but they do their best work when surrounded by others. One thing to keep in mind is that O's are not good at what they perceive to be small tasks. It is best to leave those duties to an A. And the O's will only follow rules that are in alignment with their own internal code. However, they have a superior work ethic, and they will get the job done even if it means working overtime without pay. They love people and don't want to let their colleagues down. The O's are actually a catalyst for other people's success, and are first to celebrate the accomplishments of others.

Careers

O's make great CEOs, journalists, anthropologists, psychologists, therapists, counselors, sociologists, non-profit organizers, volunteer organizers, merchants, politicians, hotel managers, film producers, media relations people, communications directors, public relations people, promotions managers, entrepreneurs, fashion consultants, venture capitalists, music producers, orchestra conductors, band leaders, translators, guides, politicians, lawyers, entertainers, writers, athletes, financial planners, business consultants, union leaders, activists, social workers, trades people, etc.

A Blood Type

Leaders

Due to their many strengths, the A blood type is a very well- respected leader in the workplace. One of the most valued characteristics of the A is their sense of integrity. This trait outshines most of their other qualities. They lead with common sense and consistency, attributes that they personally admire in others. They are tenacious, and face challenges with calm and clarity. These traits lead them to greatness. As a boss, the A gives clearly defined directives. If you are working under the A's supervision, communicate to them with equal brevity and clarity. They believe in getting to the point. Also, due to their high standards and strong work ethic, they have high expectations of their workers, which can be intimidating. However, the A leader works hard right alongside their employees, which is greatly admired by their staff. They are also known for their power of concentration, and ability to devote the time and energy needed in getting a job done right. The one area in which the A feels uncomfortable is giving speeches. The A doesn't like being the center of attention, but they will do what they must out of their sense of duty. When necessary to do so, they will make formal speeches, especially at ceremonies. As for time management, the A expects everybody to take responsibility for themselves. They are not micro-managers. They expect people to do their jobs well, and they will see the results in tangibles such as in the numbers, benchmarks and performance reviews. The A's don't like wasting time. They don't have as many meetings as other bosses because they value the time management of everyone. They are also acutely aware of their employees' needs. Their common sense gives them sensitivity to the personal conditions of their employees, and they will take these into consideration when making any decision. The A boss appears reserved, but underneath this demeanor is great warmth, humanity, and humor. The A is a leader who wins the respect of others because of their personal values of consistency, common sense, and honesty. Once you figure them out, you know that they will be the same every day, and you know what is expected of you.

Workers

The strength of an A worker is getting the job done right ~ seriously right! You can always count on the A to do a job with precision. They lay out a clearly defined plan and follow it. The A's have high standards for themselves and expect others to have the same high standards. But they are diplomats and won't point out the different work habits of others. They usually understand their position in a company and act accordingly, taking their responsibility seriously. The A's are generally rule-keepers, not rule-bender, because they think that most rules are in place in order to keep things running smoothly. The A blood type person is one who has a moral code of ethics, which include discretion, humility, and conscientiousness. They are good representatives of the company because they never act inappropriately. They are apt to be shy, and may also be quietly stubborn and serenely independent. Don't be deceived by their subdued exterior, they often have a very competitive nature. Because of their sensitivity to others, the A's will never give a direct criticism that would insult someone. Therefore, they never get themselves into trouble speaking about other co-workers. You can trust them as confidents. Because the A never boasts, their work performance can go unacknowledged at times. They quietly do the work with great efficiency, without accolades. If they have a problem at work, they keep it to themselves because they are not complainers. However, this can lead to other problems in the long run. The A might worry over details and procedures that others view unnecessary. Discussing the issues with supervisors or colleagues may relieve a lot of their stress – a condition to which an A is particularly subject. The A's are great listeners and are valued co-workers. As a team player, you can't beat an A. This is where they flourish. A co-workers are the ones that the other team members can confide in and trust implicitly.

Careers

A's makes great researchers, developers, scientists, inventors, venture capitalists, film producers, chief finance officers, financial analysts, accountants, wedding planners, estate planners, hotel managers, engineers, lawyers, law clerks, legal assistants, teachers, professors, artists, writers, editors, librarians, diplomats, orchestra members, band members, team athlctes, astronauts, veterinarians, zookeepers, marine biologists, park rangers, animal workers, mediators, writers, programmers, fashion designers, civil servants, social workers, professional organizers, librarians, social workers, tailors, architects, computer programmers, digital information managers, medical technologists, office managers, office workers, etc.

The B Blood Type

Leaders

The B's are dynamic entrepreneurs and cutting edge innovators. They make vibrant leaders who love new experiences and new products. They lead with enthusiasm and passion, with an innate interest and curiosity in everything. As leaders, they have a very easygoing and cheerful nature. There is no stopping the B when it comes to their vision of their place in the world ~ it's at the top, in the lead. Once they make a decision, they take action. When given praise they move with even greater speed. However, the wonderful thing about the B is they move forward with great conviction regardless of other people's confidence in them or approval of their project. They are the risk-takers and the trendsetters. They are able to keep an eye on their target, while ignoring the naysayers around them. The B's have the most confidence of all the blood types. What is happening in the financial world has minor impact on the B's business decisions. They go boldly forward until they decide otherwise. They don't give up on things very easily;

however, if they do change their minds, they do it swiftly, and without regret.

Workers

B's are often cheerful, humorous and interesting, creating a fun atmosphere at work. They are great communicators and express their opinions clearly. However, that doesn't mean they try to get along with others. In fact, you may not be able to gauge whether they care for other people or not, but they are really compassionate and loyal. People tend to either be drawn to them or leave them alone. They are reliable, organized workers who can be counted on to get the job done. B workers, like B leaders, excel when given praise and respect. Not because they need it to do a good job, but because they know they are doing a good job and appreciate the communication with others who can identify it. However, B's aren't known to be great team players; they work at their own pace and on their own schedule. Given their cavalier style, the B can sometimes be considered arrogant. However, the B is unlikely to be fazed by anyone's opinion of them. And, if something does affect the B at all, it's not for long; they have a wonderful way of reframing things, and gaining new insights from the situations that they confront. When all is said and done the B's are the most likely of the blood groups to get promoted in a company; charisma and performance is a hard combination to beat. A word of advice: don't tell them how to spend their money. It won't work anyway because they will do pretty much what they want. B's are free-wheelers. Their timing is definitely their own and punctuality may not be of great importance to them. However, their own pacing is purposeful and thought out in order to get their plans done. They always have the big picture in mind. At times, being on their own scheduled can lead to misunderstandings with some people and can think of the B as self-centered and unconcerned with other people's schedules. But B's are definitely caring people who love to connect with others, having a great affinity for their fellow man. They have a deep sense of loyalty; when their friends have troubles, they show compassion and empathy. The B can be very appealing due to their rich conversations and gift of humor. When a B is in the room, the atmosphere is enhanced, and they often have a magnetic effect on the opposite sex. Their temperament fluctuates because they don't hide how they're feeling. You will never have to wonder whether they like something or not. However, knowing them may not mean understanding them because B's don't' often show their deeply rooted pains.

Careers

B's make great entrepreneurs, inventors, athletes, politicians, scientists, nurse, doctors, surgeons, orchestra conductors, film directors, soloists, entertainers, journalists, public relations people, marketing people, advertising representatives, researchers, developers, etc.

The AB Blood Type

Leaders

The AB leader is rational, realistic, creative, idealistic and passionate. Their minds are chock full of ideas. They analyze everything with a special AB kind of clarity, combined with a healthy sense of skepticism and idealism. They are natural born critics. They call a spade a spade

– and they are usually right. They tend to keep things ship-shape, catalogued, and classified. Neat and tidy are the calling cards of the AB, which can be distressing to the other blood types. Their attention to detail may even border on obsession at times. An AB sees the minor things that others overlook, and sometimes they can overreact to what may seem senseless or petty to others. Part A and part B, the AB's manage their logic and emotion to varying degrees, depending upon the person. However, this characteristic can benefit a leader because they are able to see both the hard, cold facts of a venture, as well as the vision. If you are in a work relationship with the AB you may find them unpredictable at times, and may not know where they are coming from on any given day. When in the leadership role they are fast thinkers, evaluating the advantages and disadvantages of strategic maneuvers with great dexterity. AB's have a perspective on projects that may seem unrealistic to others. In fact, they do think outside the box, sometimes way outside the box. Not being swayed by anyone else's opinions, they work tirelessly towards their goals with great passion. An AB never allows others to see how hard they prepare or work at something; they prefer that others not see them sweat. They believe in coming up with results and consider that to be the ultimate statement of their worth. Despite the fact that they seem out of step with others, they have a special knack of getting along with a wide broad base of people. They have diverse friendships, which enables them to have a variety of life experiences in which they relish. However, AB's have clear boundaries, and keep a distance from others in their own unique manner. They have both the A blood type feature of being cautious, and the B blood type feature of taking risks. Their behavior changes from situation by situation, and as a leader they will do what they deem appropriate at the time. Another attribute of the AB is that they may change plans at the last minute. Although flexibility has its benefits, an AB tends to succeed more if they learn to exercise some consistency. Another annoyance for those under supervision of the AB is that they keep their own rules, even when it defies logic. And they take it a step further - they can't believe that others don't see it their way and obey their guidelines. An AB should not be judged on first appearances because they don't allow others to see their real character at first. They don't reveal their true selves until they have a situation clearly understood. Although they are generally considerate and compassionate, their other side rears its head at times, and they may say an unkind word that hurts or offends someone.

Workers

AB workers are good business people because of their unique ability to see a situation from various perspectives. The benefit of having AB workers is that they can play the role of a mediator if a conflict occurs. However, they are poor at expressing themselves and are a little bit awkward at times. They have an underlying insecurity, and a strong sense of privacy, which keep colleagues from getting too close to them. They are usually peaceful and calm, but may suddenly respond adversely. They are not driven by money, but by passion, making them great volunteers, and garnering them much respect from the people around them. When they get absorbed in their cause they may even become so driven that they actually become an annoyance to others due to their single-mindedness.

Careers

AB's make great entertainers, advertising representatives, writers, designers, business people, teachers, filmmakers, directors, orchestra conductors, negotiators, financial analysts, film/food critics, lawyers, judges, researchers, developers, etc.

Wendy Watson, C.Ht.

About The Author

Wendy Watson, C. Ht. is a Certified Hypnotherapist and Neurolinguistics Programming Practitioner. She is at the forefront of her field using her expertise in blood type and its effect on human behavior to assist clients in understanding themselves and their relationships. Wendy has spent her life exploring the human condition through the lens of limitless curiosity, endless faith, and untamed freedom. Wendy now lives in Santa Monica, California...but will go anywhere. She is an O.

www.ingramcontent.com/pod-product-compliance
Lightning Source LLC
LaVergne TN
LVHW011414080426
835511LV00005B/537